JESUS IS _____.

FIND A NEW WAY TO BE HUMAN

PARTICIPANT'S GUIDE

JUDAH SMITH

THOMAS NELSON
Since 1798

NASHVILLE   DALLAS   MEXICO CITY   RIO DE JANEIRO

Published in Nashville, Tennessee, by Thomas Nelson. Thomas Nelson is a registered trademark of Thomas Nelson, Inc.

Thomas Nelson, Inc., titles may be purchased in bulk for educational, business, fund-raising, or sales promotional use. For information, please e-mail SpecialMarkets@ThomasNelson.com.

ISBN: 978-1-4016-7807-4

Printed in the United States of America

13 14 15 16 17 QG 6 5

CONTENTS

INTRODUCTION

Jesus is _____. How would you fill in that blank?

That question is at the heart of a campaign The City Church launched a couple of years ago with the goal of getting Seattle to think about Jesus. Our purpose wasn't to tell anyone what to believe. We just wanted people to get Jesus on their minds. We gave them a chance to fill in the blank on our website, jesus-is.org, and thousands of answers came in. Some were profound. Some were hilarious. Some were spiteful. But all of them said something about the spiritual journeys of the people filling in the blank.

Who is Jesus to you? Your answer will affect how you make day-to-day decisions, how you face challenges and failures, how you love people, and how you relate to God.

The goal of this small group study guide is to help you fill in that blank by looking at what the Bible says about who Jesus is. My prayer is that Jesus will become the focus of your spiritual journey. Whether this is the first time you have ever approached this topic or you have known him for as long as you can remember, Jesus is waiting to show you more about his love, his grace, and his goodness. Jesus is a new way to live, and you are going to love the journey ahead.

An important part of this *Jesus Is* study is the small group discussions. Small groups are a great place to process the material in the book and the videos. Feel free to ask questions, discuss difficult topics, and learn from others about what God has been saying in their lives.

I would also encourage you to do your part to make your small group a safe place for everyone. That means letting other participants express their opinions, struggles, and questions without feeling as if you have to fix everyone. Jesus will take care of that—and he's better than any of us at fixing people.

By the way, this is not a curriculum about how to fix yourself, either. I'm not going to tell you areas where you need to try harder or work more. I'm just going to remind you how amazing Jesus is. How incredible his grace is. How complete your righteousness is. If I can help you keep looking at Jesus, I will have been successful. Really, it's not me anyway: pointing people to Jesus is the Holy Spirit's specialty, and we would do well to look where he's pointing.

Focusing on Jesus means thinking about who he is and what he does. It means looking at yourself less and at him more. As you read, discuss, and think about Jesus in the coming weeks, you will discover that when you focus on Jesus, loving God is easier. Loving other people is easier. Overcoming temptation and exercising self-control are easier. Life is richer, fuller, and happier.

◼ HOW TO USE THIS GUIDE

Each session will begin with a DVD clip talking about the topic for the session. Following the clip, there will be time for group discussion.

Each session also includes five mini-topics for personal study during the week. These mini-topics consist of a Bible passage, a short devotional thought, and a few questions for reflection. This is an opportunity to expand on the weekly topic during your own prayer time each day.

If you would like to write out your answers to the daily questions, space is provided in the Participant's Guide; however, this is a personal journal, and you don't need to worry about sharing your answers with others. The idea is that you take a few minutes to apply the concepts to your life, your circumstances, and your spiritual journey.

No matter where you find yourself in your relationship with God, these next few weeks are going to be a lot of fun. Jesus is your friend, your confidant, and your advocate. The closer you draw to him, the more you will enjoy his abundant life. Thank you for joining the discussion!

SCANDALOUS GRACE

Humans are doers by nature. We are constantly going, doing, working, earning, building. We are taught from childhood that if something is to be had, it must be worked for. It must be earned.

Our work ethic is a good thing, but it's no wonder we struggle to understand and accept the gift of God's grace.

Grace can be defined as God's unmerited, unearned favor. But we can't believe something as wonderful as that could be free, so we look everywhere for the strings we are convinced are attached. Surely we did something to earn this. Or maybe it was free to start with, but now God must expect something in return.

In order to benefit from God's grace the way he intends, we must learn to embrace grace for exactly what it is: free, undeserved, and unconditional.

As you watch the video and listen to the story of the prodigal son, keep something in mind. Often, in a well-meaning attempt at humility, we compare ourselves to the son in regard to our sinfulness, our rebellion, and our desperation. We focus on our waywardness and our need for God.

It's true that without God, we are lost and desperate. But that's not the main message of this story. There's another similarity between the prodigal son and each of us that is harder to spot, yet ultimately more dangerous. It's the way he related to his father. It's the tendency he had to measure his worth and his identity by his own good or bad deeds.

This is a story about grace. Scandalous, incredible, ridiculous grace. And it's a story you and I need to take to heart.

■ WATCH THE DVD

Play Session 1: Scandalous Grace

Read aloud as a group the following Scripture passages before continuing on to discussion:

- Ephesians 2:8–9

- Acts 15.11

- Romans 11:6

■ GROUP DISCUSSION

1. In Jesus' story of the prodigal son, what surprises you most about the father's reaction to his son's return?

2. Why would the father disregard cultural expectations and run toward a son who had left him as he did?

3. Do you find this story to be "scandalous," as Jesus' audience did, because someone is rewarded for bad behavior? Or is it comforting and reassuring? What does your answer reveal about your view of God's love for you?

4. How did Jesus' three stories answer the question, why does Jesus hang out with bad people?

5. Can a perfect God be wrong for loving you just as you are? What is the hardest thing for you to understand when you consider God's love and his justice?

6. In what ways have you found yourself "putting your ducks in a row" before coming to God?

7. How does it feel to hear that Jesus is like a "groupie," obsessed with you?

DAILY READINGS

■ DAY 1

For the wages of sin is death, but the free gift of God is eternal life through Christ Jesus our Lord. (Romans 6:23)

Read the scripture for today and consider:

■ Why do we typically feel the need to earn someone's gift to us, or at least pay him or her back for it somehow?

In his letter to the Romans, Paul used the word "gift" to describe what has been given to us through Jesus' sacrifice on the cross. If something has been given to us as a gift, then it is free. There is no charge, no obligation, and no debt.

A gift is a simple concept. I've never had to explain what it means to my kids. They just get it. On Christmas and birthdays, not once have they offered to reimburse me for their Lego set or football. Not once have they set the toys down, gone into the kitchen, and washed dishes until they paid off their presents.

It's grown-ups, us "mature" people, that need to be constantly reminded of the true definition of grace. It's free. It's a gift. And it's ours to keep.

■ Have you ever received a valuable gift with no strings attached? Did you feel uncomfortable accepting it? If so, why?

How would the person who gave you the gift feel if you didn't accept it unconditionally as he or she had intended?

Have you believed any wrong concepts about God's gift of grace, forgiveness, and eternal life?

DAY 2

Where sin increased, grace increased all the more. (Romans 5:20 NIV)

Read the scripture for today and consider:

According to this verse, what specific sin or amount of sin cannot be covered by grace?

This verse in Romans 5 is what some might call a dangerous verse. People might get crazy with this verse. Paul says that no matter how much our sin increases, God's grace increases even more. If our hole gets deeper, then God's shovel gets bigger. There's nothing we can do that can't be made up for by God's grace.

See what I mean? Dangerous. What's to stop me from going out and doing whatever I want? If God's grace covers it all, I can do whatever I want, right?

Actually it's more awesome than dangerous.

Grace isn't about what we can get away with. It's about a person. It's about a relationship with Jesus that doesn't depend on how well we've behaved today. When we see Jesus for who he really is, we won't abuse him: we'll embrace him.

God's grace is awesome because no matter how hard we try, we will still fall short of perfection. But every time we mess up, God's grace picks us back up and says, "You're still within my reach."

🔲 How have you seen God's grace continue to pick you up off the ground?

■ Is it possible to try too hard to be perfect? Is perfection the main thing God wants you to seek in life?

■ Do you believe that God has enough grace for all your sin for your entire life? How does your answer affect the way you live?

■ DAY 3

For God saved us and called us to live a holy life. He did this, not because we deserved it, but because that was his plan from before the beginning of time—to show us his grace through Christ Jesus. (2 Timothy 1:9)

Read the scripture for today and consider:

■ Is it difficult for you to hear that you do not deserve something— in this case, God's grace? Why or why not?

At no point during his journey did the prodigal cease being the object of his father's love. No matter how far he strayed and no matter what he did, he couldn't make his father stop loving him or looking for him.

The same goes for us with our heavenly Father. "Before the beginning of time" God planned out how he was going to show us grace. Grace always has been and always will be his intent for us. His mercies and grace "never cease" (Lamentations 3:22).

Like the prodigal son, at times we may try to distance ourselves. We may put up a fight. We may try to live independently of God. But God's love for us is based on who he is, not on who we are or how we behave. His love is relentless. His grace is compelling. His goodness breaks down our defenses.

We did nothing to deserve his love, and we can do nothing to preserve it. We simply respond to it through Jesus.

Paul wrote that "God saved us." From what did he save you? What did you do to deserve salvation?

▨ What does it mean to be holy? Should that calling be intimidating for you? How does knowing we have God's grace affect your call to a holy life?

▨ Why do you think grace was God's plan from the beginning?

■ DAY 4

You know the generous grace of our Lord Jesus Christ. Though he was rich, yet for your sakes he became poor, so that by his poverty he could make you rich. (2 Corinthians 8:9)

Read the scripture for today and consider:

▨ How does Jesus' gift of grace "make you rich"?

Jesus is God, and he existed well before the day he was conceived by the Holy Spirit in Mary's womb. He was in heaven before time began. He was there at creation, he was worshipped and praised by angels, and he had all of heaven's riches and glories at his throne.

And he gave it all up for us. He became poor by the world's standards so that we could become rich by heaven's standards. Remember, "rich" doesn't just mean having money in the bank or a convertible in the garage. It means rich in grace. Rich in righteousness. Rich in God's favor.

When Jesus died on the cross, he took the punishment for our sins so that we wouldn't have to. He took our sin upon himself, so much, in fact, that his Father had to look away. But he did it so the Father would never have to look away from us.

That is Jesus' generous grace in a nutshell.

Just as the prodigal's father didn't consider it beneath him to lift up his robe and run, Jesus did not consider that a life and death on earth were unfit for royalty like him. Is this easy or hard for you to comprehend? Why?

■ Does being a recipient of God's grace make you feel rich? Why or why not?

■ Why do you think Jesus did all that he did, giving up all that he gave up, for your sake?

■ DAY 5

Let us then approach God's throne of grace with confidence, so that we may receive mercy and find grace to help us in our time of need. (Hebrews 4:16 NIV)

Read the scripture for today and consider:

■ How would you describe the way you approach God and his grace? Is it with confidence?

When children have done something they know is wrong, parents can usually tell just by their demeanor. If you are a parent, you know this is true. You don't even have to see the thing that was broken or lost or spilled. You know something is up because suddenly, your kids are unable to approach you with confidence. Normally they ask you to buy them things constantly. They climb all over you and want to wrestle. They want to tell you every detail about their day. But now, they won't make eye contact, they won't talk to you, and they avoid you.

Why? Because they know they are guilty. Their normal boldness and expectation of favor have been replaced by a sense of impending doom.

Here's the crazy part. You probably aren't nearly as upset as they think you are. But their false perception creates a very real separation.

In today's passage, the writer of Hebrews calls us to "approach God's throne of grace with confidence." Don't run farther away. Don't settle for feeding pigs. And certainly don't stoop to eating the pigs' food. Instead, return to the Father with confidence that his grace continues to increase and that he never stopped loving us or looking out for us. There is nothing he cannot and will not forgive.

- Have you ever been hesitant to come to God and confess your sin? Why were you slow to approach him?

What would it look like for someone to approach God's throne without confidence? Does that person have a correct under-standing of grace?

What does it say about the relationship between two people when the wrongdoer can approach the other with confidence and confess? Do you have that relationship with God?

FRIEND OF SINNERS

When the people who hated Jesus wanted to accuse him of something, the best they could come up with was that he was a friend of sinners. Think about what that says to us.

First, this accusation tells us that Jesus had an amazingly holy lifestyle. Critics couldn't accuse him for his own sins, so they had to turn to the sins of those with whom he had spent time.

That's amazing. It's inspiring. And for some of us, it's a little bit depressing.

Why? Because obviously, it's too late for any of us to live a perfect life: we blew any chance we had at that shortly after we started sucking oxygen on this planet. So how can we hope to influence others?

Let me encourage you.

We can't.

Do you feel encouraged now? I'm serious, though. While we do our best to live in holiness, and while we recognize that our sin and failures have serious consequences, we can't hold ourselves up as the paradigm of righteousness. We don't tell people, "If I can do it, so can you." That only works until we fail.

Instead, we point them to Jesus. He did it, and so can we. Do you see the difference? I'm not excusing sin or encouraging complacency. I'm putting the emphasis where Jesus put it: on himself. On his holiness, his work on the cross, his gift of grace.

But that's not my main point here—that was bonus material.

The main thing the accusation against Jesus tells us is that he spent a lot of time with sinners. And he enjoyed it. He thrived on it. He looked for it.

Sure, there were times he preached from a boat to crowds on the shore. But more often than not, he was right in the middle of the crowd. People surrounded him, hugged him, touched him, tugged at his cloak, and begged him for help.

But it didn't stop there. He went to the homes of the most notorious sinners and spent the afternoon with them. That was unheard-of for any upstanding Jew, let alone for a spiritual teacher like Jesus.

As you watch the video and consider the story of Zacchaeus, ask yourself something. Would you have been Jesus' friend?

At first glance, that appears to be an absurd question. Of course we would have been his friends. Of course we would have followed him and hung on his every word. Of course we would have soaked up every minute with him. Right?

But when we take a look at who was a friend of Jesus—and who was not—the answer may not be so cut-and-dried.

Jesus was a friend of sinners—prostitutes, adulteresses, tax collectors, liars, cheaters. And they were his friends in return. They loved him. They followed him. Not because he approved of their sinful lifestyles. But because he loved them first, just as they were, and invited himself into their lives.

Do we pay more attention to the sin than we do to the sinner? Could we be accused of being a friend of sinners, as Jesus was? Do we recognize that we, too, are sinners?

■ WATCH THE DVD

Play Session 2: Friend of Sinners

Read aloud as a group the following Scripture passages before continuing on to discussion:

- Romans 5:6–8

- Romans 3:9–12

- John 7:3–38

■ GROUP DISCUSSION

1. Who do you think was more surprised to hear Jesus invite himself over to Zacchaeus' house for dinner—Zacchaeus or the crowd? Why?

2. What do you think must have affected Zacchaeus more at dinner: whatever Jesus' topic of discussion was or simply the love Jesus showed for him? Why?

3. What ultimately changed Zacchaeus's life?

4. What makes us acceptable and right before God?

5. What "trees" have you climbed in your life in an attempt to get God's attention or impress him?

6. What are you tempted to put your trust in besides Jesus?

7. What can you do this week to turn more of your attention to Jesus?

DAILY READINGS

■ DAY 1

For the Son of Man came to seek and save those who are lost. (Luke 19:10)

Read the scripture for today and consider:

■ What extreme lengths have you gone to in order to seek something that was lost?

If you have ever lost a child (or "temporarily misplaced"—that sounds better), you know what panic is. You forget everything else and start searching desperately for the missing person. You do whatever it takes. You go to any extreme.

One thing you don't do is sit down and wait for him or her to find you. That's what we teach our kids, right? "If you get lost, just stay where you are, and Daddy and Mommy will find you."

When it comes to our spiritual condition, we were lost. And while we tend to say things like "I found God," that's not how it happened.

God found us. He didn't stay in heaven, waiting for a lost humanity to find him. Jesus left heaven to seek and save us. He went to extreme measures—he even gave his life for us.

How would you describe your condition when Jesus found you? Would you have said at the time that you were lost?

Why is it hard for people—including Christians—to recognize their need to be found or rescued?

▨ Is if difficult for you to relate to spiritually lost people? Why or why not?

▨ How can you "save" people who are lost? Is it really your responsibility?

■ DAY 2

> But when the teachers of religious law who were Pharisees saw him eating with tax collectors and other sinners, they asked his disciples, "Why does he eat with such scum? When Jesus heard this, he told them, "Healthy people don't need a doctor—sick people do. I have come to call not those who think they are righteous, but those who know they are sinners." (Mark 2:16–17)

Read the scripture for today and consider:

⬛ Do you think Jesus considered those he ate with to be "scum"? How do you think he saw them?

One of our greatest challenges is to look at others through God's eyes. God doesn't see ethnicity. He doesn't see rich or poor. He doesn't see political affiliation. He doesn't care whether you wear a suit and tie or flip-flops and jeans. He's not impressed by your résumé, your SAT score, or how well your fantasy football league performed. And he's not shocked by your scandalous past or your hidden sins.

We tend to be much quicker to judge than God is because we judge based on the wrong criteria. We look on the outside—at addictions, at clothing, at tattoos, at actions—but God looks beyond all that. He just sees someone he made in his image who needs his grace and forgiveness.

That's good news for everyone—starting with us.

⬛ On what do you tend to base your opinions of others? Do you hold yourself to the same standards you hold other people?

▓ Are those who "think they are righteous" still sinners? What makes someone truly righteous?

▓ Do you judge others too quickly? Why or why not?

■ DAY 3

Jesus returned to the Mount of Olives, but early the next morning he was back again at the Temple. A crowd soon gathered, and he sat down and taught them. As he was speaking, the teachers of religious law and the Pharisees brought a woman who had been caught in the act of adultery. They put her in front of the crowd.

"Teacher," they said to Jesus, "this woman was caught in the act of adultery. The law of Moses says to stone her. What do you say?"

They were trying to trap him into saying something they could use against him, but Jesus stooped down and wrote in the dust with his finger. They kept demanding an answer, so he stood up again and said, "All right, but let the one who has never sinned throw the first stone!" Then he stooped down again and wrote in the dust.

When the accusers heard this, they slipped away one by one, beginning with the oldest, until only Jesus was left in the middle of the crowd with the woman. Then Jesus stood up again and said to the woman, "Where are your accusers? Didn't even one of them condemn you?"

"No, Lord," she said.

And Jesus said, "Neither do I. Go and sin no more." (John 8:1–11)

Read the scripture for today and consider:

How do you think God views sin and sinners? Did Jesus treat the adulteress the way you would expect God to treat a sinner?

If you were asked to pick the phrase that stands out the most from this passage, there's a good chance you would say, "Go and sin no more." It's a great, easy-to-remember quote from Jesus.

But lost in translation is the actual meaning behind the Greek, which would be better translated, "Go and leave this life of sin." Jesus was telling the adulteress to stop sleeping with men who weren't her husband.

However, what should probably stand out the most from this passage is the fact that Jesus did not condemn her; he forgave her. He did not chastise her; he set her free. In this world of judging others, gossiping, and pointing fingers, Jesus takes no part in any of it. He simply loves us, forgives us, and continues to desire relationship with us.

In this passage, Jesus clearly paid more interest to the sinner than the sin. Is it difficult for you to do the same? Why or why not?

If someone accused you, took you before Jesus, and flaunted your sins, do you imagine Jesus condemning you or defending you?

■ Who are the "accusers" that try to bring condemnation against you?

■ DAY 4

Eventually [Jesus] came to the Samaritan village of Sychar, near the field that Jacob gave to his son Joseph. Jacob's well was there; and Jesus, tired from the long walk, sat wearily beside the well about noontime. Soon a Samaritan woman came to draw water, and Jesus said to her, "Please give me a drink." He was alone at the time because his disciples had gone into the village to buy some food.

The woman was surprised, for Jews refuse to have anything to do with Samaritans. She said to Jesus, "You are a Jew, and I am a Samaritan woman. Why are you asking me for a drink?" (John 4:5–9)

Read the scripture for today and consider:

■ Have you ever made a point of showing love to someone whom most people would avoid?

"Jews refuse to have anything to do with Samaritans." It's a sad statement, but even more troubling is the fact that this sort of prejudice and narrow-mindedness still exists today. Could a similar thing be said about you, or about your friends, or about your culture?

Notice that this was no accidental meeting. Jesus intentionally stopped to rest in a city his fellow Jews would have avoided. He purposefully waited for the woman to appear. He took the initiative to begin a conversation. And he found a way to bring her into a relationship with God.

Jesus went out of his way to help someone others would have rejected without even getting to know her. He defied cultural stereotypes, ignored peer pressure, and left his own comfort zone because he knew she needed the life he offered.

■ Have you ever avoided conversation with someone who would have benefited from your company? If so, what was it you were really trying to avoid?

■ When Jesus' disciples found him again, they were shocked to see him talking with this woman. Why do you think they were surprised that he would strike up a conversation with this Samaritan woman?

How would our peers react if we stepped out of our comfort zones and intentionally sought out relationship with people our peers avoid?

■ DAY 5

Philip said, "Lord, show us the Father, and we will be satisfied."

Jesus replied, "Have I been with you all this time, Philip, and yet you still don't know who I am? Anyone who has seen me has seen the Father! So why are you asking me to show him to you? (John 14:8–9)

Read the scripture for today and consider:

■ If Jesus, the friend of sinners everywhere, is a true picture of God the Father, why do people so frequently view God as an angry, vengeful deity?

What was the main reason Jesus came to earth? Before I answer that, let me tell you what it wasn't. It wasn't to show off how holy he was. It wasn't to make us feel even worse about our sinfulness than we already do. It wasn't to insist that we get our acts together and stop sinning. It wasn't to judge bad people.

Jesus came to restore lost people to a relationship with God. When Jesus befriended Zacchaeus, it meant God himself wanted to befriend Zacchaeus. When Jesus ate dinner with sinners, it meant God wanted to eat dinner with sinners. (Side note: "Dinner with Sinners" sounds like a TV reality show . . . never mind).

When we see Jesus for who he really is, we see the Father for who he really is. He is a friend of sinners. He is a healer of the sick. He is a savior of captives. He is kind, generous, bighearted, forgiving, funny, hardworking, peaceful, passionate.

Want to know God? Want to understand how he looks upon you? Look no farther than Jesus.

▨ Why do you suppose many have in their minds two very different pictures of God the Father and Jesus the Son?

▨ Does God's view of you affect the way you value yourself? How so?

▨ Besides the list on the previous page, how would you describe Jesus and therefore God?

WITH YOU ALWAYS

When it comes to trips, some people are chronic over-packers. Chances are you either are one or are married to one.

The reasoning is "I have to be prepared for anything." That, of course, is impossible. No matter how prepared we are, something inevitably happens that wasn't on our radar. Ironically, it's often the over-packer who ends up forgetting something essential, probably because he or she was so distracted trying to plan for the unexpected.

In the grand scheme of life, we know that packing for a trip isn't that big a deal. So you forgot your toothbrush, shoes, and underwear. So you didn't put any of your liquids in the proper-size plastic bags. You'll figure something out.

But there are other times when the unpredictability of life really does matter, like when you are moving to a new city, or starting a new job, or heading off to college, or getting married.

When you're heading down a path you've never taken before, doubts can creep in. Maybe everything will work out, and maybe it won't. What if something goes wrong and you can't figure it out? What if something that you didn't plan for comes along and ruins everything? Jesus understands our need for stability, dependability, and reassurance. He lived among us and experienced our insecurity. As the eternal God, he sees the end from the beginning; he knows the future before it happens.

That is why at the end of his life on earth he told his disciples, "Be sure of this: I am with you always, even to the end of the age" (Matthew 28:20). And shortly after his ascension, he sent to earth the Holy Spirit to act as our comforter, counselor, and teacher. Through the Holy Spirit, Jesus is indeed with us always, as he promised, and we can travel through life confident that he has not abandoned us.

As you watch the video and go through this session, think about the constant presence, comfort, and guidance of the Holy Spirit in your life. Do you take full advantage of having Jesus with you always? How should your life be different from others who don't have 24/7 access to the Holy Spirit inside them?

■ WATCH THE DVD

Play Session 3: With You Always

Read aloud as a group the following Scripture passages before continuing on to discussion:

- Psalm 23:4

- John 16:33

- Romans 5:1–5

■ GROUP DISCUSSION

1. Have you ever been let down by someone who failed to live up to his or her promise? How confident are you that Jesus will always follow through with his promise to be with you?

2. When you were a child, was there an adult in your life whose mere presence made you feel confident? How do you feel when you're with someone you know you can depend on for anything?

3. Is it difficult for you to understand the Holy Spirit and his role in your life?

4. Jesus told his disciples that it would be better when he was gone, because then we would have the Holy Spirit with us always. How is that better?

5. As the video asks at the end, how would your private and public life be different if you truly lived knowing Jesus is always with you?

DAILY READINGS

■ DAY 1

The LORD is my rock, my fortress and my deliverer;
my God is my rock, in whom I take refuge.
He is my shield and the horn of my salvation, my stronghold.
(Psalm 18:2 NIV)

Read the scripture for today and consider:

▨ Whom or what do you look to the most for guidance, reassurance, support, and strength in your day-to-day life?

If you wanted to make a meal for important guests, chances are you would use a recipe from a reputable person or cookbook that has served you well in the past. Or if you needed a new suit for a once-in-a-lifetime job interview, you would probably go to a well-known store or tailor that you can trust. You don't take these situations lightly, and you want to base your choices on a trustworthy source.

When Jesus was on earth, his disciples learned to trust him. They came to understand that he always knew what was best, that he always had their good in mind, and that he kept every promise. When he came back to life after being crucified, you can imagine their joy. They expected to have him with them always.

Then he left them. One minute he was there; the next minute, he ascended into the clouds and disappeared.

But while they were still staring forlornly up at the sky, angels appeared and reminded them they were not alone. Jesus had promised to be with them always, through the Holy Spirit.

The disciples lived the rest of their lives depending on him; and now, two thousand years later, we can do the same.

Is there anything you tend to trust in during times of trouble besides God? Why?

When tough times come, how can you find strength, answers, and direction from Jesus even though he's not physically next to you?

Is the fact that Jesus is invisible a hindrance to you trusting in him? Why did he tell his disciples it was better that he leave them and send the Holy Spirit in his place?

DAY 2

For God has said,
   "I will never fail you.
   I will never abandon you."

So we can say with confidence,
   "The LORD is my helper, so I will have no fear.
   What can mere people do to me?"
      (Hebrews 13:5–6)

Read the scripture for today and consider:

How would you think and act differently if you faced every challenge with the conviction that Jesus was by your side and on your side?

There is a lot to be said for a healthy self-esteem and a sturdy self-confidence. But ultimately, they aren't enough to carry us through the uncertainties and struggles of life. Why? Because the truth is, we aren't big enough, strong enough, or clever enough to beat everything that life throws our way.

At least not on our own.

But there is someone who already beat the biggest obstacle life offers: death. His resurrection proves that no matter what we face— sin, sickness, economic collapse, relational dysfunction—we can be more than victorious through him.

I don't have life figured out. As a matter of fact, the longer I live, the less I feel that I know! But Jesus does have it figured it. And the closer I get to him, the more confident and peaceful I am, regardless of the circumstances around me.

▧ What should self-esteem mean for a Christian?

▧ Do you tend to have a poor self-image or a healthy one? How does that affect your day-to-day life?

■ When you feel as if you lack confidence in a particular situation, how do you try to bolster your confidence? Does it work?

■ DAY 3

One day Jesus said to his disciples, "Let's cross to the other side of the lake." So they got into a boat and started out. As they sailed across, Jesus settled down for a nap. But soon a fierce storm came down on the lake. The boat was filling with water, and they were in real danger.

The disciples went and woke him up, shouting, "Master, Master, we're going to drown!"

When Jesus woke up, he rebuked the wind and the raging waves. Suddenly the storm stopped and all was calm. Then he asked them, "Where is your faith?"

The disciples were terrified and amazed. "Who is this man?" they asked each other. "When he gives a command, even the wind and waves obey him!" (Luke 8:22–25)

■ What are the biggest challenges you have faced in your life? If you were a Christian at the time, how did your relationship with Jesus help you? If you were not a Christian, how would things have been different if you had known then what you know now?

You can talk about storms, read about storms, and watch movies about storms, but nothing compares to actually experiencing a storm. There is something about being at the mercy of forces beyond your control that reminds you just how small you are.

The same is true for the storms of life. Remember, Jesus never promised that our lives would be free from trouble. If anything, he made it clear that the opposite was true. Not only will we face the normal trials and difficulties of this world; we will also face persecution just because we follow Jesus.

The difference is that Jesus promises to be with us. And that changes everything.

After all, what is the worst that could happen? If we lose our earthly possessions, we have heavenly rewards that are far better. If we are ridiculed and rejected, God still accepts us. If we die young, we get to go to heaven early.

I don't mean to minimize what you may be going through. Loss is real. Pain is real. Tragedy is real.

But so is Jesus. He's even more real. And when we make him our shelter, we can weather any storm.

▦ What is the biggest difficulty you are facing right now? How does your way of handling this difficulty compare to how you would have reacted before knowing Jesus?

▦ What is the difference between the "normal" challenges of life and persecution for the sake of the gospel?

▦ How does the knowledge that Jesus is with you help you face tough times?

■ DAY 4

We can rejoice, too, when we run into problems and trials, for we know that they help us develop endurance. And endurance develops strength of character, and character strengthens our confident hope of salvation. And this hope will not lead to disappointment. For we know how dearly God loves us, because he has given us the Holy Spirit to fill our hearts with his love. (Romans 5:3–5)

Read the scripture for today and consider:

■ How does it feel when something or someone you have placed hope in lets you down? Are you reluctant to risk repeating your mistakes? Why?

We live in a warranty-happy world. Everyone wants a guarantee that the product they are purchasing is shockproof, foolproof, drop-in-the-toilet–proof, and toddler-proof. Actually, scratch that last one, because no one who has a toddler would expect that.

But if you read the fine print, you realize nothing is guaranteed to work for all time. Sooner or later, our phones break, our clothes tear, and our cars need new paint jobs.

How's this for a guarantee, though? "And this hope will not lead to disappointment." Paul is referring to the hope of salvation. We can be confident in Jesus' promises to us. He will never abandon us. He will always fight for us. He will forever love us.

Lifetime warranties are short-term compared to this.

■ How does giving us the Holy Spirit show "how dearly God loves us"?

■ Does the presence of problems and trials in our lives contradict how much he loves us? Why or why not?

■ What other guarantees of God do you rely on every day?

■ DAY 5

And we know that God causes everything to work together for the good of those who love God and are called according to his purpose for them. For God knew his people in advance, and he chose them to become like his Son, so that his Son would be the firstborn among many brothers and sisters. And having chosen them, he called them to come to him. And having called them, he gave them right standing with himself. And having given them right standing, he gave them his glory. (Romans 8:28–30)

Read the scripture for today and consider:

What would you attempt if you knew you could not fail?

Have you ever had a great idea but never acted on it because there were too many unknowns? Because you couldn't guarantee success?

In instances like these, it's not the obstacles that hold us back—it's the fear of obstacles. It's the insecurity of the unknown. If you've been in this situation but managed to overcome your anxiety and press on, you probably discovered that your fears were far worse than reality.

I'm not advocating that we do every crazy thing that pops into our heads, of course; but once we know which direction to go, we need to set doubt aside and take the next step. Jesus is with us, and he will guide us along the way.

If we follow Jesus, we really can't fail. Not in the long run, anyway. It may look like we failed, but ironically, many times our supposed failures are the doorway to our greatest successes. God has a way of using our weaknesses and mistakes to accomplish his purposes.

Most of us could stand to take ourselves a little less seriously and enjoy the grace of God a lot more. Jesus saved us when we were in the biggest mess possible—he's not going to abandon us now.

■ What fears hold you back from attempting great things?

■ Have you ever felt as though you failed at something? In the long run, did it make you a better or a worse person?

Are you excited about your future? Why or why not? Do you think Jesus is excited about it?

4

ALIVE TOGETHER

In recent years, Hollywood seems to have been overrun by zombies. Not actual zombies, of course; just movies and TV shows featuring them. Everywhere you turn, you encounter the walking dead.

Ephesians 3 describes another type of walking dead— those who are dead in sin. They don't stumble around with glazed-over eyes, trying to eat brains, which we all appreciate, but nonetheless, they are spiritually dead.

Without Jesus we can never be truly alive. Sin has a way of sucking the life out of life. It's fun for a moment, but it exacts a price we cannot pay.

Often when referring to sin, we say things like, "I'm only human" or "That's just human nature"; but in reality, there is nothing human about sin. It is an intruder, an alien, an interloper. God never designed us to sin.

Jesus came to make us truly live by eradicating sin at its source. His death delivered us instantly from the condemnation and guilt of sin. Because he gives us his righteousness, we can approach God with boldness and confidence.

We still have to resist sin, of course. Old habits die hard. But the battle has been won on a spiritual level. Even when we sin, we are no longer dead in our sin. We are alive because Jesus is alive and we were made alive in him.

■ WATCH THE DVD

Play Session 4: Alive Together

Read aloud as a group the following Scripture passages before continuing on to discussion:

- Genesis 4:6–7
- Romans 3:10–12
- John 11:25–26

■ GROUP DISCUSSION

1. What does the quote "Every man dies; but not every man truly lives" mean to you?

2. How does sin keep us from being truly alive?

3. What is the difference between accepting Jesus as a supplement and accepting him as a Savior?

4. How do we begin to lose true fulfillment and meaning in life when we allow what should be our secondary pursuits to become our primary concerns?

5. How does Jesus give us a new way to be human?

6. What does it mean when we say, "Jesus is enough"? Enough for what?

DAILY READINGS

■ DAY 1

I devoted myself to study and to explore by wisdom all that is done under heaven. What a heavy burden God has laid on men! I have seen all the things that are done under the sun; all of them are meaningless, a chasing after the wind. (Ecclesiastes 1:13–14 NIV)

Read the scripture for today and consider:

■ How much of your typical day is filled with what Solomon might call "meaningless"?

If you are feeling overly happy and would like a good dose of depression, just read Ecclesiastes. It's a guaranteed downer for your day.

I'm kidding—a little bit. This book is definitely pessimistic, or at least the first 99 percent of it is. The last two verses pull it out of its nosedive just before it crashes into a wasteland of misery.

In the book, Solomon used the words "meaningless" and "chasing after the wind" dozens of times to describe humankind's existence on earth. So what was wrong with the guy? Why was he so negative? Remember, these aren't the writings of someone who was down on his luck and had a vendetta against successful people—King Solomon was the wisest, wealthiest man who ever lived. So when he said it's all meaningless, we should pay attention.

When you read the end of the book, you get his point. Not all life is meaningless: just life without God. Solomon was saying that a life lived in pursuit of happiness and pleasure will never satisfy. Jesus came to bring us abundant life by eliminating the sin problem and reuniting us with God.

▦ Is it wrong to strive for success in your job or to obtain earthly possessions? Explain.

How are those "chasing after the wind" simply the walking dead, not really living life?

Will someone chasing after the things of this world ever be satisfied? Explain.

■ DAY 2

"Anyone who drinks this water will soon become thirsty again. But those who drink the water I give will never be thirsty again. It becomes a fresh, bubbling spring within them, giving them eternal life." (John 4:13–14)

Read the scripture for today and consider:

Where do people look for satisfaction and happiness? Why do they keep looking in the same places even when it doesn't help?

Let's go back to the story of Jesus and the Samaritan woman at the well. Jesus knew this woman was seeking happiness in all the wrong places. She had been married five times and was currently living with another man.

As she talked with Jesus and began to realize who he was, she asked him for "miracle water" so that she would never be thirsty again. She was looking for a quick fix, for temporary happiness.

She missed the point. Jesus didn't want to just give her water; he wanted to give her true peace, joy, and life.

Sometimes we get so preoccupied with the distractions, difficulties, and duties of our lives that we forget we have the source of all life with us every day. We look around for a quick fix, but what we really need is Jesus. He's not just a Sunday supplement to everything else we do. He is our source and he is our savior.

How can you relate to the Samaritan woman, who continued to look for life in the same places even though it had never worked before?

Though believers in Jesus all have the "fresh, bubbling spring," why do we sometimes look outside of Christ for purpose and fulfillment?

Are you happier when you are living a comfortable life or when you are close to Jesus?

■ DAY 3

Oh, what a miserable person I am! Who will free me from this life that is dominated by sin and death? Thank God! The answer is in Jesus Christ our Lord. So you see how it is: In my mind I really want to obey God's law, but because of my sinful nature I am a slave to sin. (Romans 7:24–25)

Read the scripture for today and consider:

▣ Does it encourage you or discourage you to hear Paul describing himself as a "miserable person" at this stage of his life? Why?

Before he met Jesus, Paul used to incarcerate and kill Christians for their beliefs. And he enjoyed it. He lived for it. He was a bad dude. By the time he wrote this passage, however, he had undergone a radical transformation. Now he was preaching Christianity all over the world, risking everything to help people know God.

So how could he possibly describe himself as a miserable person and a sinner? And the real question: if he was that bad, what hope is there for us? We may as well give up now!

Anyone attempting to live a good life can relate to the frustration in Paul's voice. I know I can. No matter how hard we try, we still end up sinning. We do our best not to, of course. And God's grace is available to help us resist. But let's be honest. We will sin at times. So if our relationship with God and our spiritual security is tied to our performance, we are setting ourselves up for failure.

That's why the answer is Jesus. He's the source of grace and wisdom to resist the act of sinning; but even more important, he already dealt with the guilt and shame of sin.

Sometimes our guilt makes us our own worst enemy because instead of running to God's throne of grace, we hide in shame. We fight sin on our own, and we lose.

But once we realize who we are in Christ, we are free to overcome day-to-day temptation from a permanent place of righteousness.

Have you ever been frustrated by your inability to eradicate sin from your life? How did you respond?

▓ Why is the fact that Jesus dealt with our guilt and shame more important than the fact that we still sin from time to time?

▓ How do guilt and condemnation actually keep us from overcoming sin?

■ DAY 4

Therefore, since we are surrounded by such a huge crowd of witnesses to the life of faith, let us strip off every weight that slows us down, especially the sin that so easily trips us up. And let us run with endurance the race God has set before us. We do this by keeping our eyes on Jesus, the champion who initiates and perfects our faith. Because of the joy awaiting him, he endured the cross,

disregarding its shame. Now he is seated in the place of honor beside God's throne. (Hebrews 12:1–2)

Read the scripture for today and consider:

- In general, do you focus more on defeating sin or loving Jesus? Which is more important?

It drives me crazy when I get a spill or a stain on my clothes. That I know would bother most people, but I take it to a whole new level. It's an obsession, a paranoia. I can't concentrate on anything until I change my outfit. And if the spot doesn't come out after washing it, I will never wear it again. I'm sorry if that bothers you—but what can I say? It's the outcome of being schooled in the art of fashion by an older sister and mother. I blame them. My quirk was bad enough when it was just me I had to worry about, but now I have three small children who take turns spilling things on themselves, on each other, on me, and on the living room furniture. I need counseling.

Many of us have a similar obsession with sin. We can't think about anything but sin. We are constantly thinking about how fun sin is, or how bad sin is, or how hard it is to resist, or how we wish we could do it but we can't, or how guilty we feel because we did it . . . you get the picture.

Don't get me wrong: I'm not advocating that we take holiness lightly or that we stop resisting temptation. But sin has been defeated by Jesus, and it's not worth all the attention we tend to give it.

Let's think more about Jesus than about sin.

How would your life change if you focused more on Jesus and less on sin?

Do you think focusing on sin could actually hinder your pursuit of holiness? Why or why not?

Would Jesus prefer that you obsess more over him or over sin? Which does he value more: your holiness or your relationship with him? How do you know?

■ DAY 5

But God, who is rich in mercy, because of His great love with which He loved us, even when we were dead in trespasses, made us alive together with Christ (by grace you have been saved), and raised us up together, and made us sit together in the heavenly places in Christ Jesus, that in the ages to come He might show the exceeding riches of His grace in His kindness toward us in Christ Jesus. (Ephesians 2:4–7 NKJV)

Read the scripture for today and consider:

■ In what ways were you "dead" before you met Jesus? In what ways is your life different now?

I'm not a fan of the zombie apocalypse genre, but I know that things typically don't work out well for the zombies. Have you noticed that? And no one feels bad for them. There is no magic cure. No antidote. No zombie rehab center. The solution to the zombie problem is always the same: they die.

As I mentioned earlier, we were walking dead people—alive in the flesh but spiritually dead because of sin. And God took the initiative to help us. Apparently, he even cares about zombies!

At the risk of overusing the zombie analogy, let me say that death is actually the solution for our problem too. Not our death, though—Jesus' death. When he died physically on the cross, our sinful nature died too. When he was raised from the dead, our spiritual self was born again, free from sin.

Because of God's rich mercy and great love, this zombie story has a good ending. We are made "alive together . . . in the heavenly places in Christ Jesus." What once was dead is now alive. Through Jesus we have a new life, a life filled with joy, purpose, forgiveness, and grace.

Are people who are "dead in their sins" usually aware of their condition?

■ What motivated God to take the initiative to step in and save humanity?

■ What did Jesus' death on the cross accomplish for you?

■ How would you describe the life that Jesus gives you?

ACCUSERS & ADVOCATES

I remember hearing about a man who had been born blind and had lived without sight his entire adult life. Over time, however, new techniques to restore sight were developed. Eventually the man underwent an operation and was able to see. For the first time in his life, he experienced color, hues, shades, and details he didn't know existed.

What surprised me the most about the story was the man's reaction to this new world. He didn't like it. He was overwhelmed by the new sensations and stimuli bombarding his senses. After a lifetime of darkness, this was too much.

Over time, the operation turned out to be unsuccessful. His blindness returned. Instead of feeling anger and disappointment, he felt relief. He was able to return to the comfort and familiarity of his limited condition.

I am sure this story does not represent most visually impaired people. But it does illustrate the human tendency to prefer the safety and comfort of the known rather than the risk and potential of the unknown.

Grace is a lot like that. When we consider the implications of a life defined by grace, of a relationship with God that depends fully on him rather than on us, we can actually feel afraid. What is going to keep people from sinning? What is going to stop people from abusing this incredible gift?

A life of grace is a new world, a world full of freedom and potential. And that makes it feel unsafe. Often we are more comfortable with law, with rules, with religion. We can control those things. We can measure them and manipulate them. With law, we always know where we stand—and where others stand, too.

But grace? It levels the playing field. Grace shows us that we all need God equally. None of us can look down on others. None of us can boast of what we have achieved.

As you watch the video and discuss the session, think about what grace means to you. Does grace frighten you? Do you find it difficult to receive? Do you have trouble showing grace to others? Is grace the defining characteristic of your walk with the Lord?

■ WATCH THE DVD

Play Session 5: Accusers & Advocates

Read aloud as a group the following Scripture passages before continuing on to discussion:

▓ John 8:1–11

▓ I John 4:17–18

▓ Romans 5:1–2

■ GROUP DISCUSSION

1. Why do you think Jesus refused to answer the question directly?

2. How do you think the woman felt upon Jesus telling her that he was not there to stone her but to set her free?

3. In what ways can you relate to the adulteress about to be stoned? In what ways can you relate to the ones about to stone her?

4. What sins in others' lives often cause you to pick up stones?

5. What makes it difficult for you to be an advocate, not an accuser, of those in your life who are doing something you may not approve of?

6. How could you better assume the role of an advocate?

DAILY READINGS

■ DAY 1

For the Kingdom of Heaven is like the landowner who went out early one morning to hire workers for his vineyard. He agreed to pay the normal daily wage and sent them out to work.

At nine o'clock in the morning he was passing through the marketplace and saw some people standing around doing nothing. So he hired them, telling them he would pay them whatever was right at the end of the day. So they went to work in the vineyard. At noon and again at three o'clock he did the same thing.

At five o'clock that afternoon he was in town again and saw some more people standing around. He asked them, "Why haven't you been working today?"

They replied, "Because no one hired us."

The landowner told them, "Then go out and join the others in my vineyard."

That evening he told the foreman to call the workers in and pay them, beginning with the last workers first. When those hired at five o'clock were paid, each received a full day's wage. When those hired first came to get their pay, they assumed they would receive more. But they, too, were paid a day's wage. When they received their pay, they protested to the owner, "Those people worked only one hour, and yet you've paid them just as much as you paid us who worked all day in the scorching heat."

He answered one of them, "Friend, I haven't been unfair! Didn't you agree to work all day for the usual wage? Take your money and go. I wanted to pay this last worker the same as you. Is it against the law for me to do what I want with my money? Should you be jealous because I am kind to others?"

So those who are last now will be first then, and those who are first will be last. (Matthew 20:1–16)

Read the scripture for today and consider:

Should people always "get what they deserve"? Do you have trouble giving or receiving grace?

I'm sure that when Jesus told this parable, people got irate. The idea that someone could work for an hour and receive the same wages as someone who had worked all day would have messed with their sense of justice just as it does ours.

Our whole lives we are taught that we get what we deserve; that if something is worth having, it's worth working for; that if we want anything, it's up to us to make it happen. Don't misunderstand: a healthy work ethic is important. But when our pride in our efforts keeps us from recognizing our need for grace, something is wrong.

Let me just say it: grace isn't fair. We tend to embrace that when we are the ones who need grace, but it makes us mad when it's the other guy.

In reality, we can never be good enough to make up for our bad deeds. Romans 6:23 says, "The wages of sin is death." So if God operated on the basis of fairness, we would all be in trouble.

But he doesn't. He shows us grace.

▦ Does grace seem unfair to you? Why or why not?

▦ How did Jesus' death fulfill the wages of sin?

▦ What things do people do to try to pay for their sin?

■ DAY 2

> But God demonstrates his own love for us in this: While we were still sinners, Christ died for us. (Romans 5:8 NIV)

Read the scripture for today and consider:

■ Why would Jesus die for sinners?

When Christmas season rolls around, most of us know who we are going to get presents for. We have a list of who gets a big present, who gets a small present, and who just gets a card. That list, whether it's written or mental, says a lot about our relationship with those people. For those close to us, such as our spouse and children, we are willing to buy the best present we can afford—sometimes more than we can afford. We give extravagantly because we have a close relationship. We trust those who are close to us. We know they love us.

But what about people who don't know us? Or people who dislike us? We certainly don't buy them extravagant gifts—we probably don't even send them cards.

That's not how Jesus operates, though. While we were still strangers, while we were still enemies, before we had even thought about him, Jesus purchased the most extravagant gift possible: eternal life. He expected nothing in return.

Now that we know him and love him, we don't need to hide the fact that we are sinners. We don't need to put up a false front. Jesus knew exactly who we were when he went to the cross, and he loved us just the same.

▓ Have you ever been wildly passionate about something or someone? How did you show that passion?

▓ Do you find it reassuring to know that Jesus died for you even knowing that you were a sinner? Explain.

Why do we sometimes try to hide our sinfulness from God?

■ DAY 3

When people work, their wages are not a gift, but something they have earned. But people are counted as righteous, not because of their work, but because of their faith in God who forgives sinners. (Romans 4:4–5)

Read the scripture for today and consider:

Would you rather earn something or have it given to you as a gift? Explain.

How in the world could I ever be considered righteous? If that question crossed your mind as you read today's passage, you would not be alone. Maybe you've never even been exactly sure what *righteous* means, but you knew it didn't pertain to you. Jesus, definitely. Billy Graham, maybe. You? Not a chance.

If you need a little help understanding the word, *Merriam-Webster's Collegiate Dictionary* gives us a pretty good definition: "free from guilt or sin." Notice it doesn't say *without* guilt or sin, but simply *free* from it.

We are free from the guilt Satan tries to lay on us because of our sin. Free from the punishment our sin deserves. Free because Jesus, the Righteous One, paid the wages for it with his death. And because of his sacrifice—not our work—we are counted as righteous through faith in God.

Yes, there is satisfaction in earning wages through work, and there is a time and place for hard work and for claiming rewards. But this amazing gift of grace and forgiveness could never be earned. Instead, the God who loves us more than we can imagine gave it to us freely and with no strings attached.

Is it difficult for you to receive an extravagant gift, especially from someone you could never repay?

What is most difficult for you to comprehend about your right-eousness before God?

How might you live differently if you saw yourself as God sees you?

■ DAY 4

"I have come that they may have life, and that they may have it more abundantly." (John 10:10 NKJV)

Read the scripture for today and consider:

What does the world say an abundant life looks like?

Everyone reading this has life. And if you've placed your faith in Jesus for forgiveness from your sins, you have eternal life.

But what about an abundant life? Do you think Jesus had more in mind than spending eternity in heaven when he spoke of giving us life "more abundantly"?

Imagine a man who owns a thousand acres of rolling hills, luscious green meadows, and beautiful forests. If all he does with his land is build a five-hundred-square-foot home and never leave his front yard, does he still own the thousand acres? Absolutely. But he's not enjoying it. He's not benefiting from its resources. He's not exploring its beauty. He's not living life abundantly.

Jesus offers us so much more than what most people dream of. His abundant life includes physical things, like food and clothing, but it goes far beyond that. He gives us forgiveness. He gives us relation-ship with God. He gives us righteousness, peace, and joy. He gives us freedom.

Are you taking full advantage of this gift?

How is Jesus' idea of an abundant life different from the world's idea?

▦ In what areas are you living an abundant life?

▦ How could you be living life "more abundantly"?

■ DAY 5

Under the old covenant, the priest stands and ministers before the altar day after day, offering the same sacrifices again and again, which can never take away sins. But our High Priest offered himself to God as a single sacrifice for sins, good for all time. . . . For by that one offering he forever made perfect those who are being made holy. (Hebrews 10:11–12, 14)

Read the scripture for today and consider:

▓ Why do you think God instructed the high priests to offer sacrifices if they could never take away sins?

Baseball is a depressing sport, at least if you're a perfectionist. Your goal is to hit a three-inch-wide ball that is travelling at ninety miles per hour, using a stick just barely wider than the ball. Even the best hitters in the world miss 70 percent of the time.

Now imagine a six-year-old T-ball player stepping up to face those same pitches. He can try all he wants, but he will never hit a pitch. If by some miracle the bat does connect with the ball, the poor kid is probably going to go flying farther than the ball.

The priests of the Old Testament were like that T-ball player, only not so lucky. They offered the same sacrifices for sins day after day, but it was never enough. That's not a criticism of them, because they were doing what God commanded. But no animal sacrifice could ever be sufficient to pay the high price of sin.

But then Jesus came. He was the ultimate High Priest, and he offered himself as "a single sacrifice . . . good for all time."

Jesus hit the ball out of the park. He won the game when he dealt with sin once and for all.

▨ Why do we continue to focus so much on sin, even though our debt has been paid and it is no longer an issue for us as believers?

▨ If the sacrifices made by the Old Testament priests were inadequate to deal with sin permanently, why did they keep offering them?

▨ What does the fact that Jesus was a sacrifice "good for all time" mean for your melding past, present, and future sins?

6

COUNT THE WAYS

Sometimes when my kids want to talk me into something, their strategy is to tell me how much they deserve it: they got an A on a science test, or they won a football game, or they cleaned their room.

I love their enthusiasm, and I often give them what they are asking for. But most of the time, I don't give them what they are begging for because they earned it—I give it to them because I love them. They may think they talked me into it, but in reality, I love to make them happy. I'm looking for excuses to give them treats and surprises. My love for them predisposes me to be generous toward them, whether they deserve it or not.

More often than I care to admit, I find myself trying to talk God into blessing me. I tell him how much I love him. I tell him how wonderful he is. I tell him how good a person I've been lately. All of it is calculated to influence God in my favor.

I'm sure he appreciates my enthusiasm, too. But he really doesn't need me to talk him into being good to me. That's his nature. That's his passion and joy.

When Mary and Martha appealed to Jesus to come heal their brother, they understood this principle. That's why they didn't list out all the reasons Jesus should come. They didn't try to lay a guilt trip on him, or flatter him, or manipulate him. They simply said, "The one you love is sick." That was all that mattered.

If you find yourself in need of God's help in a particular area, take a minute to reflect on his love for you. Remember that he is pre-disposed to help you. Consider that he knows the situation from start to finish. He has your best interests at heart.

No matter who you are or what you have done, there is no way for him to love you more than he already does. As you watch the video and discuss the session, think about what it means to be un-conditionally loved by Jesus.

■ WATCH THE DVD

Play Session 6: Count the Ways

Read aloud as a group the following Scripture passages before continuing on to discussion:

- John 11:1–44

- 1 John 4:7–10

- Romans 5:8–11

■ GROUP DISCUSSION

1. Mary's and Martha's first response upon Lazarus becoming so ill was to send for Jesus. Is he usually your first response in times of crisis? What other things or people might we turn to first?

2. How does it feel when you know you are loved by someone?

3. Where outside of Jesus do we tend to look for love? How does that love compare to the love of Jesus?

4. Do you ever find yourself trying to convince God to be good to you? What does that say about your concept of God?

5. In the heated moments of our lives, Jesus and his love for us should occupy our thoughts. But what other things sometimes slip in and take precedence?

6. What are some ways that God shows us his love?

DAILY READINGS

■ DAY 1

And I pray that you, being rooted and established in love, may have power, together with all the saints, to grasp how wide and long and high and deep is the love of Christ, and to know this love that surpasses knowledge—that you may be filled to the measure of all the fullness of God. (Ephesians 3:17–19 NIV)

Read the scripture for today and consider:

▨ Is it humanly possible to comprehend the love of Jesus? What is the best human analogy you can think of to describe Jesus' love?

The love of Jesus cannot be measured because it never runs out. It has no limits or conditions. As Paul wrote, it truly "surpasses knowledge."

At the same time, Paul prayed that we would "know this love." How can we know something that surpasses knowledge? It's simple: by experiencing it.

It's impossible to quantify or define the love we feel for our parents, for our best friend, for our spouses, or for our children, but we know it's real. Similarly, but on a much larger scale, we can receive and revel in Jesus' love even though it surpasses our comprehension.

We experience God's love every time we go through difficult times. We experience it when he speaks to our hearts and directs our decisions. We experience it in prayer, in the Word, in worship, and even in fellowship with other Christians.

The love of Jesus is invisible and intangible, yet it's the most real thing in our lives. Long after this world is gone, his love will remain.

▓ What did Paul mean when he said we were "rooted and estab-lished in love"?

▓ What does it mean to be "filled to the measure of all the fullness of God"?

▓ Think about what is most unlovable about you. Why does Jesus still love you as he does?

DAY 2

> God showed how much he loved us by sending his one and only Son into the world so that we might have eternal life through him. This is real love—not that we loved God, but that he loved us and sent his Son as a sacrifice to take away our sins. (1 John 4:9–10)

Read the scripture for today and consider:

How is God's love better than our love? Why was sending his Son to earth the ultimate demonstration of God's love?

As John wrote above, our relationship with God is not about our love for him. It's about His love for us.

Sometimes life has a way of making us question if God loves us. Difficult seasons come, our prayers seem unanswered, and we wonder if God even cares.

If we ever needed proof of God's love, all we have to do is consider the gift he gave us in Jesus. Even if God were to never do anything else for us, that one gift would be more than enough to demonstrate his heart.

As I mentioned earlier, our gifts say something about our relationship with someone. They tell the recipient, "This is how much I love you." With his gift, God is showing us once and for all that he loves us beyond comprehension. He gave us the best; he paid the ultimate price. Why? So he could bring us back into relationship with him.

The giving doesn't stop with Jesus, of course—God gives us abundant blessings in every area of life. But nothing will ever compare to the gift of his Son, Jesus, and eternal life through him.

- When someone gives you an amazing gift that shows how much he or she truly loves you, how do you typically respond? What does it do for your relationship?

- Have you ever wondered if God abandoned you or stopped caring for you?

How does the gift of Jesus and eternal life through him put our present difficulties in perspective?

■ DAY 3

"Greater love has no one than this, than to lay down one's life for his friends. You are My friends if you do whatever I command you. No longer do I call you servants, for a servant does not know what his master is doing; but I have called you friends, for all things that I heard from My Father I have made known to you." (John 15:13–15 NKJV)

Read the scripture for today and consider:

What would you be willing to do for your best friend?

When Lazarus was sick, his sisters sent for Jesus because he was their friend. Their confidence and boldness came from their relationship. Jesus didn't get upset that he had to travel to where they were. He wasn't irritated because their emergency messed up his schedule. He would do anything for his friends.

Jesus calls us his friends, too. Think about that. Jesus—God incarnate, Savior of the world, perfect in every way—is our friend. And because of that, he willingly left his throne in heaven to live on earth and be crucified as a criminal. He gave his life for us—his friends.

Wish you had friends in high places? It doesn't get any higher than this.

How important is friendship in your life? Would your best friend be willing to die for you? Would you be willing to die for him or her?

You probably view Jesus as your Lord, Savior, Creator, and God. Do you also view him as a friend? What dimensions does that add to your relationship with him?

■ If Jesus viewed you as a friend worth dying for, what does that say about who you are?

 DAY 4

"... the disciple whom Jesus loved ..." (John 13:23; 20:2; 21:7, 20 NIV)

Read the scripture for today and consider:

■ Did Jesus love any of his disciples more than the others?

In case you were wondering, the mysterious "disciple whom Jesus loved" mentioned by John is none other than John himself. His self-appointed title sounds a little arrogant. Really, John? Are you the only one he loves? Are you the one he loves the most?

Actually I find his attitude fascinating. John figured out a secret we would do well to learn: our identity is wrapped up in Jesus' love for us. Rather than seeing ourselves through the filter of how much the world loves us, or how much our parents love us, or how much our boss loves us, we should look to Jesus for our self-image. We should define ourselves based on his opinion of us.

Personally, I think I'm Jesus' favorite. I really do. I happen to believe that Jesus is passionate about me, that he can't stop thinking about me, and that he loves to spend time with me.

And I think you should think the same thing about yourself.

Was John arrogant to describe himself the way he did? Explain.

How can looking to others outside of Jesus to define our value be detrimental to our self-worth?

How will seeing yourself as "Jesus' favorite" change the way you live?

■ DAY 5

How great is the love the Father has lavished on us, that we should be called children of God! And that is what we are! (1 John 3:1 NIV)

Read the scripture for today and consider:

What does it mean to be "children of God"?

Someone who has been adopted into a family has, according to the law, been given all the rights and privileges of any blood children in the family. It's not a trial run. It's not a temporary arrangement. The adoptee has become the child of the adopter.

That is what God has done for us. We are now officially his children through the grace that Jesus brings us. God is our Father and Jesus is our brother, and nothing can break that bond.

As I've mentioned before, God took the initiative to rescue us. He found us when we were still sinners. We were in a state of animosity, denial, and rejection of him. Yet he loved us so much that he made a way for us to be adopted into the greatest family ever: the family of God.

Now, we belong. We are accepted. We are welcome. We measure up. Not because of our works, of course, but because of the righteousness of Jesus. And now that we are his children, how much more will he care for us, cherish us, and even spoil us?

- Do you feel worthy to be called God's child? Does he find you worthy of it? Explain the difference.

- What rights and privileges are offered to you as a child of God?

How does it feel to know that you are in God's family and that you belong there?

7

WITH US AND FOR US

In the last session we talked about how Mary and Martha sent for Jesus when their brother, Lazarus, was very ill. They said, "He whom you love is sick" (John 11:3 NKJV).

Jesus loved Lazarus; but inexplicably, he stayed where he was two more days. Why would he do that? Can you imagine what Mary and Martha endured during those two days as they watched their brother's life fade?

After the two days, Jesus went to their house and performed a very public, very remarkable miracle: he raised Lazarus from the dead. I'm sure in that instant, the days of suffering and pain that the sisters suffered were forgotten in the joy of seeing their brother restored.

We can look at the results and realize that Jesus' plan was bigger and better than just healing an illness. When it comes to getting people's attention, a resurrection trumps a healing any day of the week. But ultimately, we don't know all the reasons why Jesus waited those two days any more than we understand all the work and the timing of God in our own lives. I remind myself on a regular basis that God is God and I am not, and that is a good thing.

What stands out the most to me in this story is not Jesus' power. It's his compassion and empathy for the human condition. When Mary and Martha suffered, Jesus suffered. When they rejoiced, he rejoiced. He knew exactly what he was going to do—he even told the disciples about his plans beforehand—yet he still wept with the sisters.

As you watch the video and discuss this session, think about the heartaches in your life. Think about the painful times and the losses you've experienced or are experiencing. Are there areas in your life where God seems to be waiting too long to rescue you? Do you believe that God is both *with* you and *for* you?

Be assured that he has not forgotten you. He has not abandoned you. He has not given up on you. He feels your pain and he weeps with you. But it doesn't stop there: he has a plan for your victory that surpasses anything you could imagine.

WATCH THE DVD

Play Session 7: With Us And For Us

Read aloud as a group the following Scripture passages before continuing on to discussion:

- Jeremiah 29:11

- Psalm 23:1–4

- Romans 5:1–5

■ GROUP DISCUSSION

1. Why is Jesus with us? Why did he make the promise to always be with us?

2. What does it mean that Jesus is "for us"?

3. If God is for us, then those who are against us should really be a minor issue. But why do we let the people and things that oppose us become bigger obstacles than they really are?

4. How have you seen God taking the difficult experiences in your life and working them together for good?

5. How can tomorrow be different for you knowing that whatever it brings, Jesus is both with you and for you?

DAILY READINGS

■ DAY 1

What shall we say about such wonderful things as these? If God is for us, who can ever be against us? Since he did not spare even his own Son but gave him up for us all, won't he also give us everything else? (Romans 8:31–32)

Read the scripture for today and consider:

■ When you were a child, did you believe that your parents, grand-parents, or other family members would do anything within their power to help you? How did they show sacrificial love?

Sports fans love to brag about their teams and argue with fans of rival teams about why their team is better. But no matter whose team has the most all-stars, the fastest runners, or the highest scorers, one argument will always trump all others: "Scoreboard." In other words, look at the score. Look at the stats. Look at the season record. Say whatever you want about how great your team is, but take a look at whose team finished with the most points, and the argument is over.

The same could be said about a God who "did not spare even his own Son" for us. Does God love us? Does God desire relationship with us? Is there anything God wouldn't do for us?

He gave his own Son. Scoreboard.

Have you ever felt that God is against you or has deserted you? Why? Was it a correct conclusion?

How can God's gift of his only Son trump all arguments against God, especially during times of crisis?

What could the "everything else" that Romans 8:31–32 describes mean for your life? What does God want to provide for you?

■ DAY 2

"I have told you all this so that you may have peace in me. Here on earth you will have many trials and sorrows. But take heart, because I have overcome the world." (John 16:33)

Read the scripture for today and consider:

■ What does Jesus say is more important than the "many trials and sorrows" we will have while on earth?

At first glance, John 16:33 might lead us to believe that Jesus frowns upon those in sorrow and expects people to be happy no matter what the situation. That is far from the case.

Jesus understands sorrow. He knows what heartache and loss feel like. In fact, in John 11, when his friend Lazarus died, even though he knew he was about to raise Lazarus from the dead, Jesus wept with real sadness. He cried because others were crying. He mourned because others mourned. Death and suffering were not God's intention when he created humankind, and their existence brings him sorrow.

Sin, suffering, and death do not have the final word, however. Jesus proved that in his resurrection. He defeated every enemy, and now we are free to "have peace" and "take heart" even when life is tough. Through Jesus, we can find hope in sadness, joy in mourning, and life in death.

How has Jesus "overcome the world"?

What makes it difficult for you to find peace in times of turmoil?

Life can be hard at times, but what can we look forward to as our ultimate reward after this life is over?

■ DAY 3

> Consider it pure joy, my brothers, whenever you face trials of many kinds, because you know that the testing of your faith develops perseverance. Perseverance must finish its work so that you may be mature and complete, not lacking anything. (James 1:2–4 NIV)

Read the scripture for today and consider:

■ Have you seen any trials in your life develop perseverance and other forms of maturity in you?

The phrase "pure joy" brings to mind different ideas depending on who you are. Maybe for you, a newborn baby would be pure joy. Or maybe retirement. Or a house with a view of the ocean. Or acceptance into the master's program you are applying for. Or signing with a record label.

It is unlikely that anybody would define pure joy as the trials he or she faces, though. We avoid trials. We dislike suffering. We do everything in our power to stop pain.

In this passage, James wasn't telling us to seek suffering for the sake of suffering. That would be weird. Rather, it's the classic good news/bad news scenario. The bad news: suffering, trials, and pain will come. The good news: when you know Jesus, even the worst things life throws at you end up helping you. Because of his grace, the things that would destroy most people simply make us better people.

We can rejoice even in tough times because we know that God is taking something meant for evil and using it for good.

How can someone who has endured pain and loss come out stronger than someone who hasn't experienced such difficulties?

What are the most difficult types of trials for you to persevere through and see God working in?

▓ Have you ever experienced something that at first seemed to be a catastrophe but ended up being just what you needed?

■ DAY 4

For the law was given through Moses, but God's unfailing love and faithfulness came through Jesus Christ. (John 1:17)

Read the scripture for today and consider:

▓ Does God always look on us with favor? Can we make him stop loving us?

One of the things that can most hinder our walk with God is our perception of his countenance toward us. We know that he is always with us, but what if he is mad at us? I don't know about you, but if he's ticked off at me, the thought of him nearby is not very comforting!

It's important to remember that God isn't just with us—he is for us. He thinks we are amazing. He is madly in love with us. He can't stop thinking about us, talking about us, bragging about us.

But sometimes, our guilt and condemnation get in the way and we don't see that. We just know that we yelled at the neighbor again this morning, or we had another lustful thought, or we said something

WITH US AND FOR US

hurtful to our parents. We assume that God is about to drop the hammer. Sure, he's been patient with us so far; but this was probably the last straw.

That's not the case. He's not mad at us. Even when he has to step in and deal with sin, it's not with a scowl on his face or disgust in his voice. He treats us with compassion and seeks our good.

I'll say it again: God is with and God is for us. When we imagine his face, we should imagine him smiling at us, cheering for us, and celebrating us.

- What picture do you have in your mind of God? Does that picture change depending on your performance or behavior?

- What does God think about you when you have sinned?

- Is it easy for you to imagine God celebrating you? Why or why not?

■ DAY 5

Can anything ever separate us from Christ's love? Does it mean he no longer loves us if we have trouble or calamity, or are persecuted, or hungry, or destitute, or in danger, or threatened with death? (As the Scriptures say, "For your sake we are killed every day; we are being slaughtered like sheep.") No, despite all these things, overwhelming victory is ours through Christ, who loved us.

And I am convinced that nothing can ever separate us from God's love. Neither death nor life, neither angels nor demons, neither our fears for today nor our worries about tomorrow—not even the powers of hell can separate us from God's love. No power in the sky above or in the earth below—indeed, nothing in all creation will ever be able to separate us from the love of God that is revealed in Christ Jesus our Lord. (Romans 8:35–39)

Read the scripture for today and consider:

■ What is your greatest fear? How does the knowledge that God loves you help you deal with that fear?

If you were to make a list of all the bad things that could happen to you, you might feel a bit overwhelmed. I don't recommend it, actually. It would be an endless and depressing exercise. There is simply no way to foresee, much less protect yourself against, every possible difficulty.

Paul knew that. In this passage, he listed a few of the things that his readers were facing. Chances are you are facing some of these obstacles plus a few more that aren't mentioned.

How did Paul encourage his readers? Not by frantically telling them how to overcome each obstacle. Instead, he gave them the bigger picture. "Nothing in all creation will ever be able to separate us from the love of God that is revealed in Christ Jesus our Lord."

That pretty much sums it up. No matter what you are facing now, regardless of what might be waiting around the next corner, you can be at peace. God's love will always be there for you, and that's all that really matters.

▦ When we consider all the suffering in the world, how can we still say confidently that we have been given "overwhelming victory"?

▓ Though "not even the powers of hell can separate us from God's love," that doesn't mean they don't try. Are there circumstances in your life right now that make you feel as though God's love has failed? Has it failed?

▓ How did Jesus reveal God's love for us? Do you find it easier to believe in God's love when you look at Jesus' life?

LIVE LIKE YOU'RE RIGHTEOUS

You probably don't need me to tell you this, but the day after Thanksgiving is called Black Friday. It's one of the busiest shopping days of the year in the United States. Ironically, this day of frantic shopping falls the day after we sit around and talk about how thankful we are for what we have.

It's called "Black" because it's crazy. Chaotic. Frenzied. It's when otherwise reasonable, dignified people find themselves camping outside a department store in freezing weather. Then the doors open, and they try to beat out seven million other people for a few giant TVs and some flannel pajamas. The rush on the door is like the running of the bulls in Spain, only more dangerous.

115

There's nothing wrong with shopping for sales, of course. And if you enjoy extreme sports like Black Friday, more power to you. I'm just poking fun at it because it's a bit of a commentary on human nature. The hyped-up sales, the flashing lights, the giant signs—they promise a lot, but they usually disappoint. The doorbusters run out. The lines are long. The sales are limited to a few items.

Two thousand years ago, Jesus invented something far better than Black Friday. We call it Good Friday, and it was the day he died on the cross for our sins. Hardly "good" for him, but it was the best thing that could have ever happened to us.

Through his death and resurrection, Jesus gave us a gift that never gets outdated, that never needs replaced, that never runs out. His gift is truly free—no strings attached. And his gift is available for everyone, not just the first in line.

His gift is forgiveness. His gift is righteousness. His gift is grace.

■ WATCH THE DVD

Play Session 8: Live Like You're Righteous

Read aloud as a group the following Scripture passages before continuing on to discussion:

- I Corinthians 15:12–20

- Romans 5:18–19

- Colossians 3:1–4

■ GROUP DISCUSSION

1. Thinking of the chocolate bunny analogy, what does a "hollow" faith look like?

2. Why does it matter if Jesus rose from the dead or not?

3. What does it mean that we've been transformed from the inside and given a new nature?

4. How can it be true that we are no longer sinners by definition when obviously we still all sin?

5. What does it mean to live *from* who Jesus made us, not *for* who Jesus wants us to be?

DAILY READINGS

■ DAY 1

Since you have been raised to new life with Christ, set your sights on the realities of heaven, where Christ sits in the place of honor at God's right hand. Think about the things of heaven, not the things of earth. For you died to this life, and your real life is hidden with Christ in God. And when Christ, who is your life, is revealed to the whole world, you will share in all his glory. (Colossians 3:1–4)

Read the scripture for today and consider:

▦ What does it mean to think about the things of heaven?

Sometimes we think God's biggest goals for us all have to do with sin: Stop sinning. Stop wishing you could sin. Stop even thinking about sin.

So we try our hardest to stop. We strive and strain and stress, but it's no use. The harder we try to stop thinking about something, the more we focus on it.

Here is the amazing point of this passage: if we died and were raised with Christ, then holiness is not about us. It's about Jesus. We are free to focus on him, to think about heavenly things, to concentrate on enjoying our right standing before God.

This passage is not about struggling to ignore the things of earth. It's not about trying harder. It's not about gritting our teeth and avoiding sin. That is not God's primary concern, and it should not be ours. Pure living is important, but it is a natural by-product of our walk with Jesus.

Loving Jesus, not avoiding sin, is the focal point of our lives.

▦ What are God's primary goals for us?

▨ Why is it hard to focus more on Jesus than on our weaknesses and sins?

▨ In what way is pure living a by-product of our walk with Jesus?

■ DAY 2

So just as sin ruled over all people and brought them to death, now God's wonderful grace rules instead, giving us right standing with God and resulting in eternal life through Jesus Christ our Lord. (Romans 5:21)

Read the scripture for today and consider:

▪ Can both sin and grace rule over the same person at the same time? Explain.

Human approval is a fickle thing. One minute people think we are heroes; the next minute we make a wrong move and now we're villains. We're never sure if we are loved or hated or somewhere in between.

So to be told that we have been given "right standing with God" at all times just doesn't compute. *How can that be? This was a bad day for me. I lost a lot of sin battles today. I can't possibly have the same standing with God as I did yesterday, when I was overcoming temptation and praying and reading the Bible.*

Yet it is true. Sin does not rule over us anymore; God's grace does. That doesn't mean we never sin, but it means grace covers our sin completely, all the time, leaving us in right standing with God.

▨ Do you ever project your insecurities regarding human approval on God? That is, do you think God has the same opinion of you that other people do? How is his opinion of you different?

▨ Why is it so difficult to adjust to a grace-ruled life?

▨ How can your relationship with God be better today knowing you are always in right standing with him?

■ DAY 3

For if you are trying to make yourselves right with God by keeping the law, you have been cut off from Christ! You have fallen away from God's grace. (Galatians 5:4)

Read the scripture for today and consider:

■ How do we get right with God? By grace, by good works, or both?

Years ago, if someone would have asked me what could cut me off from Jesus, I probably would have said, "Sin, of course."

I would have been wrong.

Now, I'm against sin. Sin is wrong. Sin is bad. Sin is what put Jesus on the cross. But sin is not what cuts us off from Christ.

How are we cut off from Christ? According to the Bible, it is by trying to be justified by the law. That should make us stop and think. We like to think that keeping the law is what makes us better in God's eyes. It makes him love us more. We get brownie points in heaven, and when we need something, we can cash in those brownie points.

But living by works actually alienates us from Jesus. That's what the Bible says. We can't trust both Jesus and works for our salvation.

Either we stand by grace or we don't. Either Jesus' work on the cross was sufficient or it wasn't.

I'm talking to myself, by the way—for some reason, it's way too easy for me to tell God, "Thanks for the salvation. You can take a break now. I've got it from here."

Don't stoop to living by law when you are already living by grace.

Does doing good make us more righteous in God's eyes? Why or why not?

What happens to grace when we try to make ourselves righteous with our works?

▨ Do you ever find yourself thinking that you were saved by grace initially but now you have to maintain your holiness by good works?

 DAY 4

We know we love God's children if we love God and obey his commandments. Loving God means keeping his commandments, and really, that isn't difficult. For every child of God defeats this evil world by trusting Christ to give the victory. And the ones who win this battle against the world are the ones who believe that Jesus is the Son of God. (1 John 5:2–5)

Read the scripture for today and consider:

▨ How difficult is it to overcome sin, to please God, and to remain in his love?

I'm not going to lie—I'm a competitive person. I like to win and I hate to lose.

We all know what it's like to play a game where the teams are so lopsided that it isn't even a competition, where the outcome is decided before you even begin.

It's a lousy feeling to be on the losing side. To feel as if no matter what you do, or how hard you try, or how well you perform, you're never going to win. Not even close.

When you are on the winning team, however, everything is different. You know that no matter what, your teammates will carry you to victory. Your mistakes don't really affect the outcome of the game. Your performance is only secondary. With no risk of losing, you are free to enjoy the experience.

When it comes to sin versus righteousness, the competition isn't even close. We don't have to wonder if we'll conquer sin and please God, because the game is rigged. Sin doesn't stand a chance. The outcome is already decided. The God who created the universe is on your team, and whoever is on his team wins. Now you're free to enjoy the experience.

- How important is our performance in the struggle to live in holiness? What happens if we mess up?

■ Who is the star player on our team?

■ Why does sin seem like such a big opponent sometimes? Does sin still seem big when compared to God?

■ DAY 5

"Heaven is my throne,
　　and the earth is my footstool." (Isaiah 66:1)

Read the scripture for today and consider:

■ Why is God's perspective so different from ours?

You can usually spot worried people from a long way off. They are the ones pacing, fidgeting, checking their phones every few seconds, and jumping at every sound. One thing they are *not* doing is sitting down with their feet kicked up on a stool.

How do you imagine Jesus in heaven? As he watches what is going on down below, is he stalking to and fro, wringing his hands? Or is he sitting on his throne with everything under control?

This passage in Isaiah paints a humorous picture. Jesus is sitting on his throne, and the earth is his footstool, his ottoman. That's how big and powerful and sovereign he is. I imagine him with his throne reclined a bit, his arms behind his head, and his feet propped up on the earth. All is well with the world, because Jesus knows who is on the throne—he is.

When stress and worry come your way, when the world brings everything it has against you, picture Jesus sitting down in heaven, relaxing through it all. Then take a seat yourself. Everything is under his control. Let Jesus handle it.

▦ Why does it make us feel better to try to take control of a situation?

Why is Jesus able to relax even though sin still affects the world?

What good does it do to worry about the future? How does the fact that Jesus is calm and in control help you stay calm?